AMERICAN BARRICADE

YESYES BOOKS *PORTLAND*

DANNIEL *SCHOONEBEEK*

AMERICAN BARRICADE

CONTENTS

ONE

TWO

THREE

Remember come evening the last hatch of mayflies

I have lit what's left of my life

ONE

GENEALOGY

Men loyal first off to silence run in my family.
Ask about the women we say women.
What a scream. Ask about the men we say.
Men loyal only to stillness run in my family.
Not the same, you understand, as when a man.
Who refuses to budge withdraws into himself.
As when one wounds a tree to draw its sap.
Only to find the bucket come evening is empty.
Men of such stillness you hear us pulse.
Loyal to nothing like my father whose father.
Was a man who when he saw himself said.
I am too small. Too small within this world.
And too full of talk. My life I would live.
Could I live as a potato bug loves, beating.
Myself into the ground when I need you.
Then comes the sun and draws its cutlass.
And Opa's tongue the first off to silence.
Story I learned my father wouldn't tell me.
For though he was a man who couldn't read.
Music, he still found a way to write it, his life.
A short movement composed solely of rests.
Two sons he had two summers far too loud.

Now I am finished with my strings, he says.
Enough hammer, enough sustain, the end.
Men loyal first off to sustenance or sentence.
Ask about the women we say what women.
We have are women who have nothing.
There is my brother leading a horse whose.
Hunger is so loud it shakes the earth shakes.
The trees and when the apples fall he eats.
If she feeds he feeds her only from his knife.
If she rides he rides her only when he leaves.
There is me. Loyal only to when I tell myself.
That boy who has written across his wrist.
I'm god would make a good son but only if his.
Voice is a silence in which now I appear.
Ask about his mother he says mother.
Let her rip. Men who mean something.
Different than you when they say we.
Are loyal first off to the end, to the end.

DEBUT

The suit I wore the day I was born

I stole
from a thrift store was wove

out of very cheap mother
warm muslin

I soiled
like men do

when the day comes to ruin their threads

FAMILY ALBUM

I. First words

God's hooks
mother goose help son

peel you

those russets he's frothing
to strain you

a name

from his pile of skins
Deborah Jean

MY LIFE IN ABSENTIA

Some say the mother of gone to the dogs.
Others our lady of thanks for nothing.
One swears on all the fillings in his head
he saw the goddess of pickpocketing
fatten his only friend on fool's gold and next
in the saga of rotten hands, I was dealt
my life in the heart of a pocket-watch heist.
I'm told I take after father with my full head
of rust. I'm told one day the choke leaves
wouldn't leave the tree, but the man who
brought his hatchet brought home kindling.
I hear history such as *this* one calls his youth.
One calls his friends the ones who high
on the fire tower I hear impersonate him.
When one of them tastes my name on his
tongue they say he vomits out of violation
alone (and trespass, and scorn) and madder
root is all his mother buys him for the burn.
I hurl myself here and there, but only on days
I wake up with a mouthful of coins and look
at him do you see him spitting up all his
change, my friends say. Next I say

I fell, though I know full well I was kicked
into love with a girl whose eyes were
the color of riptide. I never understood
I say, what people meant when they spoke
of how hard a woman's face can grow,
but then my brokest summer in the field,
when my hunger was such that I planted
my rags, she brought me a flask of gunpowder
tea so hot it burned my lips—despite even, I say
that the sun was having its way with me.
The following winter I vowed, as you know,
that if I could not erase the crow's foot
from her face, I would throw my life away
like a rock thrown through a pile of snow.
When my father found this out he shot me,
once, a look like he wished he had shot me,
and landed me a job remaindering debts.
And I do. In my hands his troubles don't
endure. In my hands I hold my boss,
whose hands I touch now more than father's,
and when the two are the same man standing
behind me in the doorway, who can say if those
are not the days I steal most from the company.

FAMILY ALBUM

II. Moving day

Bless you 1915

& bless

mister Schiele

he stroked

son a house with

red shingles

Let's live here

ten years

eat crow

& starve

in our attic

Son's brother

mum father

sis the goat

& the basset

they snored

head to toe

like kings

in their single

MYTH

I am a natural wonder of crumbs in the beard of a third generation immigrant son of a
dentist who failed to tunnel his way out of America with a spoon

I am a natural wonder of split ends and holes in her shoes my mother born in that decade
of parents whose love was fired by bickering and no diploma for you

I am a natural wonder beneath the live oaks we aspire and fail to eradicate with our limbs
the sun they say then my sister brings her child to light like a sleuth

I am a natural wonder of waiting for my brother to crumble who like myself has survived
himself thus far on a diet of gristle and peeling the skin off his childhood

I am a natural wonder my friends die in holes a man made of ribbons my country hired he
handed them a shovel in the desert he said dig if you want to do good

I am a natural wonder I watch through a keyhole the woman who forged but won't patent
me extinguish my name on her tongue like a matchstick one lifetime too soon

I am a natural wonder will you weep when I go down in history my puttering engines will
you blame me if my plane goes down in the sea in the sun in the dogfight

FAMILY ALBUM

III. First kiss

Mother

tucking
son under

the covers

& whistles
all this

deadbolt

night making
room for

mosquitoes

ANALYSIS (RORSCHACH)

All : in his throat he tried to think of everyone whose life was a shambles that night

this : he thought of mother alone in her kitchen drinking a glass of boiling water it helps

deadbolt : her swallow the fistful of keys she found in the tackle box she buried behind

night : the house the keys thin as needles she takes them into her mouth they unlock her

making : tongue she takes them into her throat they unlock each bolt they unfasten each

room : clasp and land inside her like coins hitting the pit of a well he thinks that's mother

for : ever the pinchfist she will bury her keys when she hacks them back up she will name

mosquitoes : each one after the men in her life who handed her the keys to their shambles

FAMILY ALBUM

IV. Exemplar

It's painless pop
warns son

just shoot boy of mine
for the hole

but snags
on the gold teeth

when pop wolfs
his pink

savagery back down
his stone

washed jeans' throat
Fuck *me*

you're a sharp
shooter

with a phd in piss
now son

POEM FOR FOUR YEARS

Waiting for her to finish washing her face off and mother

who was king to me in those days
in her fur
and her robe dragging behind her

found me waiting for her to find me and saying to myself

the curse word
I learned that
summer in daycare I couldn't define it for her

she said my full name and in this house the word we say when we want to say

that word is blank
do you understand me

Like the kings in my books already I could see the worms laying claim to her face

Her expression
blank so I named it

my curse year and think of her now and wonder which was her first and want to

blank myself
in the quavering dew of summer

as mother

would have had me   say it

•

Of the lessons I learned my wunderkind year there was

god defeats king my mother is god

that's the king's dirt in my mouth

that's god's soap in my mouth

that's not how we talk in this house

My friends are monsters they come in a box they die when mom knocks

That isn't mom

mom doesn't knock

A rest is when a song observes silence a blank if you will

There is the long rest four knocks

There is the quaver

often it feels over before the beat starts

As a child climbing out of the washtub the lice

in my scalp the suds

in my mouth I thought   this is not time enough

I chose a measure of fifty-two rests

I learned that
if I turned my head and shook out the dirt and looked at the song

it even resembled a bed

so I named it my rest year instead

•

When god woke me up it was sweeps again
the season
finale the fifth season

She said I loved this man the moment I met him it was the first season he emerged from
    the wreckage his family in ribbons

I said my god comedy

is when you demolish a building

to build from its rubble

a building   and tragedy

is when you demolish a building

because apart from rubble

it wants to be nothing   and you

can go blank yourself
she said

She said the man I love emerged with no father the first season silenced him a rest do
    you hear me a blank

I love him despite him
once a year disappearing

I love him despite

and now the finale the man she loves dies he succumbs to the light he was major to me
    she cries the major key to my minor

And the weather inside her no name for it

it's like the eschaton
minus the trumpets
but with more cicadas more tinnitus

The song when it seeps at the end is the wrong song not enough rests she says

She says I want to return
to the first season when everyone's poorly

lit and the man I loved I don't know
if I love yet

I say mother think of the long rest   spring summer fall winter

four knocks

Mother why does this fifth season
disappoint us so

is it because my king   spring summer fall winter we don't have a name for the weather

Blank yourself
she said

and I named the fifth season nothing
and I named it my sweeps year again

•

It's true
the sun has since ended

The king she's canceled
the sky

And now when I leave the grounds my people they call me a figurehead
a mouthpiece
a straw boss

The oxblood robe
they say

he refuses to drag it behind him he refuses

our king her inheritor

The wind inside its canceled quiver rests   The nothing season is here

I say my people

an insult is when I must rise to the name you call me

must demolish it must
build a new name from its rubble

or else rubble

is the name I was born with

My people if it's true my name is Straw Prince and I'm guilty of my beard

my god I will shave
my throat in the quavering

my god it will glint like a hatchet blade

My shoes
I will line them up like two rests

My collar as white as my skin I will wear it around my neck

my stockade

With these four knocks if it's true I must leave the kingdom in search of a mother

to mother the child I don't

owe my people

I will walk until I come to a slum lord

She will starve
the lice in her fur

and slum lord I will tell her

I want to blank
your face

With these trumpets burning holes in the sky our king canceled
and my family
beside me in ribbons

in this nothing season slum lord when I wander your streets and they quaver and eschaton

slum lord I feel louder

I feel louder each morning spitting your rests from my mouth I feel louder
than the worms
laying claim to your face

I enlist and entrust

my bones to a traitorous cause now and slum lord

I feel louder than your dead who inherit the crown I feel louder

than their dead's dead's dead's
dead's dead

In this nothing season

with your blank
in my mouth
with the lice

in my scalp I will hunt for a mother to mother my child and name it

my loudest
year yet

FAMILY ALBUM

V. Bull market

No son's friends were
militia they shipped
in a box son built
them a brothel it was
death not a furlough

HIS INDUCTION

My oath is I'll die with my hand on the oxford bible
My president's name on my tongue like the last town I sacked

•

I'll fall on my sword so well I'll put Rome to shame
I'll wait for your donkeys to crazy and trample me home

•

Your men will tattoo my face on their feet when they war dance
Your women will stitch my name in their linens and soil them

•

Each town you name in my honor you'll name smithereens
Each elm you plant me will wilt me a portrait of leaves

•

And when it's your turn to kiss the rings of the bone thief
And when Manhattan is dross and piled with grave goods

•

I'll death so well they'll say dying is ripping me off
I'll finger my name on your tongue like it was your first born

FAMILY ALBUM

VI. Wunderkind

That's a troubling

number of woodlouses
passing out

leaflets
beneath
son's flagstone

& ocktoong! son says
my loyal

countrymen of the dirt

ick been
Straw Prince

(my friends call me god)

that's the god of rough
housing to you

to be honest don't

let son catch you
asleep
on the clock

NECTARINES

In my youth	with my two front teeth
in my pocket	I was a man of obscene wealth
I owned a pissed mattress	her grease stains
and worn patches	the bedbugs inside her
they worshipped me	I had a spell of shingles
measles too	a rash spelled my name on my arm
I wore my red eyes proudly	I flaunted my blisters
I rode a cat named Dusty	nineteen pounds he dragged
his paunch in the dirt	and stunk up the house like bad fruit
I had a very expensive sister	Tiffany Laurel I named her
She had a navel so big	I dreamed I would drown inside
and ketchup stains rice cake crumbs	she could never rid
from her blouse	If I scrape the plaque from my teeth
and think of her now	I'm sucking the pit of a nectarine
I'm tearing the pulp from the clingstone	and sucking another
Her face like a word problem	I answered wrong and erased
until what was left	but a smudge of dead skin and charcoal
that left a smear	as bright as a wound on the page
If I think of her walls	they were lined with black cork
will I teach myself	how a man wears a hole through his body
like he's beating a snare	with a hickory stick
If I hear her in the next room	push in the thumb tack

and finger the navel   of Janet Jackson whose poster
she hung on her wall   the face worn away
and behind her a man   he's holding the pits
the nectarines I didn't know   I wanted to suck yet

•

That was the year   the boy named Billy happened
Billy with his face   like a fruit bat wearing white face
Billy with his tongue   that liked to slop up nectar
In her bedroom I heard him   disappear himself
inside my sister   The wetness in her whimper
he smothered   like boiled silver was weeping
from her mouth   We have a Billy problem
I said to the bedbugs   the blisters the shingles
that spelled out   his name on my arm

•

And one by one they deserted me   The grease stains the piss
they dried on the mattress   My red eyes snuck off in the night
Even the faithful cat   I found him licking the dirt
from his paunch in the sun   and guarding her bedroom door
And Billy with his face   like a dead tomcat's asshole
Billy with his problems   and his very expensive teeth
Billy with his tongue   that slopped the plaque from sister

lapped the stains   the rice cake crumbs from her blouse
licked inside to her nectarines   and sucked at the pits
What else could I do but tear you Billy   It was her birthday
Tiffany Laurel was off   shaving her legs in the river
I tore you from the wall   erased your snared mouth
wore a hole   through your face's white pulp
Billy with your two front teeth   in my pocket
I laid myself on your body   I pissed myself
I tore the white pulp beneath me   tore Janet Jackson
and left you on sister's bed   a pile of moist cremains
Father when he found me   the piss on my hands
the nectarine juice   leaking from the hole
where my two front teeth   were missing
he built me a raft of crayfish   and banished me down the river

•

Well I'm a broke man now Billy   The crayfish below me
they're drowning   but each morning they ask for a story
I tell them the one from my youth   what she looked like that day
my very expensive sister   watching from the shore
the crumbs in her hair   Tiffany Laurel I named her
the ketchup stains on her blouse   the nectarine pits
hidden beneath the cotton   and my god the silver Billy
I swear I can taste it   that silver that poured from her mouth

FAMILY ALBUM

VII. Mumps

Wet nurse says check
the boy's vitals:
his cat died of worms
he swore off god
by this time son was 16%
made of silence

IVORY

You're a runt with a mouth more foul than gash father told me

You're a curse word
for dirt

You're worse

You're the sulfur water I pump from the well

that I drink so I won't
die thirsty

The darkest you piss

you'll piss on my legacy
you'll spit

in the shoes they strap to my hooves when they bury me

(Like a grease ant
roaming the fringe of the village

for scraps

he bottoms out
our wagon at the foot of the mountain

& turning out his pockets curses the thoroughfare)

I'm filthier
than the milk money

he shoves in my mouth he tells me my progeny

my breed
my litter

must learn cursive

& fitness
& weltschmerz

& leaves me
to practice mad minutes at the academy

•

You're a slackjawed chigger who don't belong nowhere he told me

my fitness
instructor with two blown-out hips

who plopped
three of the pale girls I loved

like a feast in his lap

I struck a pact with myself on the field that morning where boys

with black eyes & red noses
stole flags & stuffed turf

into the mouths of their opponents

If Jessie Lynne or Crystal or Melinda Anne
don't love us

by the time the last bell rings today

like a thief ant
scouring the fields

for a heist

we'll walk the fringe of the village we'll feed on the mites

We'll wait for a woman
like oil

to strike us rich
to unearth us

& hold us aloft to the sun

•

But nobody told me

the first time I said a man with lowbred vocabulary

when a woman with deathly pale hands

asked me who am I
that it'd feel like pointing a boot knife at her under the table

& feel like plucking the silver

out of her teeth
& feel like shaving my face with father's black canines

& sloughing the skin off

& denying
the refuse was me

•

I fled east to the ivory city

where the queen of the harvester mites
with skin in her mouth

indentured me

I studied the bones of the debutantes

their pale skulls

until I could taste my voice inside them saying

swagbellied girl
come home to my basin & wash out my mouth with your soap

With my blade I'll carve you
a castle of leftover ivory

where there are no curse words no sulfur no boys & no legacies

I can taste my voice
where it fouls your skull

I can taste it like lye
on your fingers

Here in the kingdom
I'm carving you

we've no fields
no pacts here no flags

Only weltschmerz & fathers & women I love & the harvest

FAMILY ALBUM

VIII. Birthday

Father's plucking
five pellets

& each tweeze

from son's cheek
pop's dropping

his buckshot

tink tink in the basin

INSCRIPTION (VAULT)

When you dig us back up

and the last fires dying on the western rim

I want one of you

to say in your language
god's hooks

what a fine set of teeth she had

I want one of you
to snap from my neck

the harmonica I wore from a thread

(if it helps think of me
a deserter

say I've come to remove his dog tags)

Now I want you to hold it above you
against the wind

(I want there to still be wind)

and the one who's not dancing

when the song

issues forth

I want him to sing

in your language god's hooks remember

this was their song

not ours

I'm singing

this was their wind that fights its way through the teeth

TWO

ITINERARY (NEW COLOSSUS)

One dream I have is the voice of the statue is gunfire.
Mother calls, the landlord calls—the line is silent.
I watch myself decompose in the mirror a minute.
I check for bites. I check nothing's left of the oats.
I wait for a word to appear in my alphabet soup.
My friends swoop down like owls and fly into the wall.
Tell me what I owe, and screech, and fly into the wall.
I wash myself and think how mother dressed a wound.
I dress myself and think how father cleaned a fish.
Heidegger tells me three dangers threaten thinking:
one I call liberty, one I call oats, one I call what I owe.
Soon the landlord will come and admire my soot.
His heaps, he wonders, which of his heaps will he bless?
His hand inside my hand is like holding a handful
of poppies, or a handkerchief a child dipped in milk.
When I leave I'll count the women without children.
If I don't I'll count their children's broken guns.
The train to work will stall beneath the river.
I'll try not to say how close the end of self comes:
like a handful of poppies, or the bowl they rest in,
or the water filling them both—each possesses
nothing the water coming through the window won't.

Soon I have a dream I take the city down with me.

I strike the name of my company from the building.

A friend writes the word *wisteria* and disappears.

The elevator falls a story—I use this word *god.*

A man I've met introduces himself and collapses.

Soon the bees forget. Soon the colony collapses.

I tell one of the workers to tell me how she works.

How I work is my business, she says, and collapses.

Home I undress how my father rinses an apple.

I rinse my mouth how my mother undresses a man.

The play I see is the man playing me collapses.

The woman I see is the voice of a gun when it backfires.

One dream I have is you visit me, Emma Lazarus.

One must bless his heaps is all you'll tell me.

One I call colony, one I call soon, one I call what collapses.

FAMILY ALBUM

IX. Tycoon

Fever dream in his hand me down skivs is a red stork airlifts son a new brother

I'm rich
son yips
can we
keep him
can son
name him
Erik no
Derek no
better yet
Pay Dirt
no son
wants to
name brother
Oil Derrick
the stork

barking yes

& scooping
a dollop
of crude
from son's blackhead

WORK'S END

You don't cement
me the ratty
girl of Polish
blood yawps
like a freak
at her brother

I'm the cement

& weak bones
pink eye
the boy
whomping it
his red cement
truck into
the pavement
I pour *you*
he putters well why
do the bags
they're white
& stabbed
like kills
on the gates

hang dead
why do hogs
no matter
where I live
exhaust me
Josie I entered
my railroad
tonight said
enough
& trying
on the gold
bolt lock
to fuck
a few
knuckles up
saw you
wear boots
to the waiting
room Hervé
Guibert a book
you've never
read in your hand
the original
diary the line

like idea

for a letter

to D. *listen*

whetstone

it's my silence

paving me

inside your

red silence

CORRECTION

The question of whether the idea of America is dead is not a question.

A question by its definition does not cease to exist in the language.

You hear spoken by those who ask it. This is why the dead, if we say.

Where the living belong are the dead, are not a question. Think of a fire.

Eating its way across a battlefield. Breathing the air for which the dead.

No longer exist. Think of it searching the field for a good place to die.

The question of whether the fire is dead is not a question, as the question.

Of whether the fire is alive still exists in the language you hear spoken.

By those who ask it. This is why in America the idea of a fire is you eat.

More air than the dead can expire or else the earth you can't stomach.

Devours you too. In America the idea of a fire is what you consume.

Is where you belong. Which is why where the earth belongs is the dead.

And why the only good place to die is where the idea of a fire does not.

Cease to exist in the language you hear spoken by those who ask it.

•

Now my brother waits for me on the other side of the river

Watching the shadow factory
burn to the ground

Once he called across to ask if I worry

is a man catching fire

without warning

all you think we inherit from our father

And I told him to say it once more in our language

Before this year

is done he said

do I wake up at the end of town

is my body thrown

through the windshield of my car

Which is when the country will long to say *I'm finished*

When all that's ours

is all a man leaves us

and all we continue is his reign over dirt

Which is when my brother will cross the river

Like a fire eating its way across a battlefield

How I wonder he'll say

if a family is waiting for me

a few years down the road

FAMILY ALBUM

X. Pax americana

Death's favorite hick
with dead

tooth son wore
suede
dumpster shoes

& hawked
Old Golds

to the local mosquitoes
to quote

the 15 year old sister of the first duchess
son loved *son yours*

is a beautiful dick O son

was busted up
in those days for his pop

whom we had
to forgive
for ratifying him

BILDUNGSROMAN (SPARE AMERICAN)

Ist sommer? sommer war

—Paul Celan

Sunburned as he was and salt in his beard and fucked

he stood here South Street
the edge of the sea

Counting the breakers off Liberty Island

he's dying for it
his licorice and whiskey

A family the father in seersucker the child in seersucker

they wave to him
from the ferry

They throw their coins in the water they pass in front of the statue

Nobody asks
where is mother

He stood here he counted
his earnings

(nineteen seventy
nineteen years old

and nobody's father
It was the year

of the hard hat riot on the steps of city hall

year he cut
his beard and begs

to help hammer in the window of the world's

tallest building)

where today I stood
with the world's

poorest woman her hair like the hay

in the town my father discovered
when he saw it was time

to refuse to keep painting

and fucking and die

Sunstruck as I am and shorn and the world's poorest woman beside me

will we marry

will we family

Two thousand nine

thirty-nine years after my father threw down his wage

swears he must quit his job

or his whiskey

and keep painting and fucking or die

Is it summer

If the lawmen come on horseback

and the seagulls

tear up his money

forgiven by only itself

will the old sea buckle

FAMILY ALBUM

XI. Independence day

In my gasoline town
it's bats

slow & whiter

than thunder claps

help us shriek home
our cattle

each dusk

& bless us son says

with mom's
stolen perfume bottle

we won't forget to
mistake

them for choughs

WHEN A THIEF DIES

At last the young
face away from the capitol

•

Now out
hiss the gaslamps

like a young
girl's spit

on the grill

•

I'm a young whore I put out my eyes
the better

to interrogate the rich

•

And shingles of cries
and yips

they fly from the roofs

•

Now laugh with me fools

•

It's the titans who turn their backs on your paychecks

WHOLE FOODS

Officers please
should you
see a man
shoot past
you hair
on fire
what skin
he has left
it peels
off his back
like cheese
cloth a pitch
fork stuck
in each thigh
and bag
after white
plastic bag
our Swiss
ruby chard
our swollen
mangosteens
our chicory

root his

rutabagas

the Humboldt

Fog he loves

his Black

Forest worms

our yellow

and red ones

our good

Korean pears

his goat's

milk gouda

his pignolis

olives so fat

you could

smother

your child

to sleep

with one all

units you

see him fire

our wild rice

from his sawed

off shotgun

pour nectar
down his
throat and chant
in some dead
language what
to your ears
you'd swear
it was lines
one and two
you learned
by heart
in grade
school man's
first no
the fruit of
disobedience
that fair
tree the last
word who
speaks it
a black sleet
in god's
land to wipe
out the kings

the line

how does

the line end

the night

who will

the night end

FAMILY ALBUM

XII. Firebrand

American podunk
god with jock itch his famously

lothario

heart of sawdust which once
chewed a rival
oil tycoon's
lust for conquest
straight south
to the quick
of his fraidy cat
ancestors' pubes

son gathers here with his bullhorn in line with the jobless
& protests

our pink slips our cheekbones our pickaxes namesakes our lock picks

& worst of all
the smoldering looks

to which our pops
couldn't help but betroth us

LEDGER (DELAWARE BOYS)

One of us falls into the manure spreader the sun
have you seen it

it bleaches the straw
the bone meal

It watches the flies in hysteria defile what's breathing or isn't

They breed
They hatch

The field like the thigh of a horse we think it trembles

Have you seen it the sun it smears
the salve in its eyes

It strikes out pitiless   and burning the shit

•

Osmon Steele undersheriff of Delaware County he wore the tin on his heart
He boasted

during the Anti-Rent War eighteen forty-five that lead cannot

penetrate Steele
Well the bullet

when it ate through the six-pointed star on his shirt

was the black tooth
of an appaloosa it tore through the badge it left

a hole the size of a solar eclipse

A man in calico dress and tin horns on his head he wouldn't admit he fired

the shot
(stifling that august

inside the courtroom) his testimony

he said Osmon was a good man a Delaware boy and so
the casket closed on him

He said justice for me is a field of dead horses in summer the flies when they come

they think themselves ghosts
They think it's winter

But the ones who rent your land we know better it's tar

not flies
and that isn't snow it's feathers

•

August in Delaware County the days do not end

not until a spinach seed
or a Delaware boy

pushes his hand through the earth

We say we'll dust off
the book when we find it here in the dirt

its cover like skin   if skin is blue corn

We say here in our American Legion
when the sandlot is empty

we will find the book and settle our names that we could not settle like scores

One of us didn't know it
was loaded

One of us when he tore his shirt he soaked the strips in ether

He breathed until
he saw the million larvae

hatch in each of his eyes

One of us is shot down
in the desert the fire was friendly they ship him back home

wrapped in horse meat and feathers the sun

strikes out pitiless

and burning the quills

One of us we hear say I saw one of ours one of the Delaware girls today

Her face it was smeared

it was rouge on her face and unguent like one of those Bedford girls

I quit my mouth he says

like I'd quit any field that yielded no harvest one of us

instead of a fist inside of a rib cage was built with a boot knife inside of a rat cage

One of us bit

into an earthworm went crazy he chases

his father whose face

he's never seen

down a gravel road dragging a string of empties behind him

The casket is closed man

we hear one of us say

The words in his skull we can see them glinting like coins

the manure spreader the grinder

the blades and the bone meal the sun

it's burning the shit

The casket is closed man we don't pay
respect we don't

shake his father's hand we don't kiss his mother's

When we find the book

we will settle our names that we could not settle (we say it) like debts

•

We say when his hand

pushes its way through the earth
I will pay Osmon Steele

the two silver dollars I stole from my grandmother's eyelids

Thank you for the horses landlord
Thank you for the shit

I will tear my shirt to dress his wound I will smear the salve where the flies crawl
into his eyes

Osmon they breed
They hatch Osmon

They strike out pitiless   and tarring the skin

FAMILY ALBUM

XIII. Allowance

A shame
son won
a slow
county
sow not
his sister
sow lows
to taste
a man so
bad son
feeds her
his milk
money

THIMBLERIGGER

My god can he hide a nickel.

My god his tooth is gold and like a bullet.

And do you see the way the coin.

When he touches its face disappears.

And if he takes my hands, which I was saving.

If I place them on his table, which collapses.

It is almost too bright now, this setting.

This west where I have still not heard my numbers.

It is almost Black Friday.

And may I thank you for the ticket that wins nothing.

For the bag of mint too rotten to eat.

May I thank you for your death, and for your clothing.

Now, when it's almost never closing.

When the door disappears, and the siren begins.

And my god if I could push my way past you.

FAMILY ALBUM

XIV. Manhunt

Night the crispness of counterfeit money

son's elm
like a bad wife

is stripped
in public

I'm shamed with her limbs
to her knots

she says as she scrapes past
son's window

I'm shame
that feels for its leaves in the dark

LITTLE WHEEL

So. The god comes for me with a hole in her négligée.
And I throw her out of the bedroom and finish my tea.
So ends the scene that begins when I write you a history.
The tea, it is gunpowder. The bedroom, it represents me.
The history is one of men boarding up their windows.
And here comes Mayakovsky kicking his hole in the wall.
He hands me his boot and his father's sawed-off shotgun.
Bite yrself off! he screams. *Fire what lives in belly represents* you.
I say, don't you see all this gunpowder tea I'm drinking.
I say, why do you think I barricade the bedroom, Vlady.
And he finds my cleanest shirt and tears off the sleeves.
Not enough holes, he says. *Now a few words about me:*
Beyond wall, is trenches. Beyond trenches—is jackals.
Tell Lily, he says. *I am waiting like child for my haircut.*
Tell her I wait in bedroom and worship her like bombshell.
And he shows me the hole where he lost his first roulette.
And I throw him out of the bedroom and finish my tea.
So ends the scene that begins with no way out of history.
I worship a hole in the wall. The wall, it represents me.
The history is one of men plotting against a little wheel.
One bet means orphans. One means neighbors of zero.
One bet means men throwing themselves out of windows.

And all this time you are failing to write your love poem.

You are waiting like a child for a word superior to *me.*

You are finding what's left of the tea too bitter to finish.

The god you refuse, she stands at your door and smokes.

The hole you worship is false. False as a god and it closes.

So. You take stock of your inheritance: shotgun, fire, boot.

Then your belongings too: gunpowder, barricade, sleeves.

So ends the scene that begins when you say I am history.

SPIDER VEIN

I swear my old
lady some night
when I dial her
& damn the eyes
of the lawman
who keeps her
thin jobless no
alimony & high
all her summers
it's her no class
podunk accent
I won't make out
over the sough
of the white
blood snowing
inside her

FAMILY ALBUM

XV. Alimony

Then pop disappeared

it was summer

son axed a slit

in the breaker

& made for the border

ALIBI (HONEYLOCUST)

I told you already   I came to your bankrupt
city with the white   root of a turnip rotting
in my pocket   and no needle and thread
to my name   Scratch down your plea
you remember   Scratch down your plea
the paperboy said   And he handed me a rock
and a lost head nail   I told you already
Sweet nothing and my plea   that's all I wrote
Sweet nothing   if you will come stumbling
out of your one story house   how a bee
stumbles out   of a bluebell sweet nothing
you remember your toothache   I will blow
my cigar smoke   into your mouth
What cigar the boy said   and he skipped my rock
across the lake   where the others lay I remember
there were nickels   where his knuckles were
missing I remember black bags   were caught
in the honeylocust branches   like what happens
to flies when flypaper   happens I told you
already: smoke   And when the skywriter wrote
everything must go   there was no one standing
on the corner of Evergreen   and I wanted

a love I could break like a dollar   and still
without love, spend   Then you people appeared
You found me I told you   The dogs blew away
their nametags their teeth   You asked me how
it was possible   how I survived the explosion
You remember how little   you had you had
little chunks of bone   stuck like buckshot
in your face   and a penny where your eye
was missing   What explosion I said
and you told me   I picked up my torch

THREE

LULLABY (COUP)

- One word is all
  - you're allowed
    - when you
    - come to rule
      - fool through
        - the fool
        - after him
      - the gate
  - to take with you
    - the state
      - he took
        - he took you
      - king
    - the first

TELEGRAM

Then father sent for me when the sky above his America was failing to thunder.
Unbroken thing he said looking up you're the color of everything exploded at once.
Unbroken thing I drink your moonshine I wake at daybreak when you catch fire.
And mother she watched too like she was watching a skin heal across her soup.
Start your machine she told father else I'll leave you how a verdict leaves a plea.
Unbroken thing he said I will show you the face you show those who worship you.
Unbroken thing I will dig you a hole I will fill it with water I will give you a vanity.
Then mother left it was summer she gathered her miniatures and made for the border.
The field was like static the mosquitoes everywhere in love or at war with each other.
And father for fifteen years with his machine he dug his hole and he filled it with water.
Unbroken thing he said the sky I've built does a better impression of you than you.
Unbroken thing and my wife and my thunder and where have you placed my America.
I will send for my child he will sing me a torch song I will send for his hollow-body.
Instrument his father in his fifteen years as a failed revolutionary did not touch.
Did not string did not tune nor clean the body did not carry upon his shoulders *stop*.
Now father sends for me when the sky above my America declares bankruptcy.
Unbroken thing he says child you'll walk to the hole I dug with my machine.
Unbroken thing you bring a foxglove you place it where it breaks the water's skin.
Child kneel down to your face where it ripples and whisper *in thunders ends the voice*.
This machine I brought you here to build will destroy me because it isn't a machine.
And the voice with which you break the skin the sky above your America can't stop.

FAMILY ALBUM

XVI. Town hall

Our dark
horse our son
the one
no one dares
to call
stalking horse
rides a mule
of 100%
cow's blood

People of destruction
derby I give you

my candidacy & unleashes

son's pups
& barks in the bullhorn

my opponent is history

& history
is what's coming
to wash
his mouth out with gas

A WOMAN IN THE SUN

The shed behind the barn behind the red cottage I wait

for her in the fescue grass the rye I hear it grow over me

Wait for my friends in the distance on fire their full heads

of rust (*I love how the clothing drips off them* I hear myself say)

If the beekeeper doesn't come chasing behind with a hatchet

I'll wait behind Cobb's barn watching the distant houses

She will come down this road my shadow is paving for her

a stalk of honey and the rye grass grows from her arms

(She was raised in these hills looking down on Elk Creek)

and behind her the bluegrass it's reaching to touch her ankle

ULITSKAYA

Not far
if you leave

my city there's forest.

A man fat
scarf
ushanka
stub of
pencil
in his teeth.

In the snow stamps his boots studies blueprints.

It's his beard
what betrays

he's the news.

We want roads & roads
will be
built you can
wager
your life
on that crust

he writes.

Next police.

Police in the snow sip their tea tell jokes about women in night clothes.

The thick
hairs with his
herringbone
beard comb
the whiskered
one brushes
down flat

next bludgeons

the news man
like weeding
his garden
six knocks
on his skull's
white clacker
guess what.

Write story that's we want roads & roads will be built that's a bludgeoning.

Beat so

well for life

he won't

piss nor

inhale burnt

coffee's

the story she's telling New York while you funnel your paycheck

into my savings

the man

with his shoes

blacked nice says & worms

his two

fingers

& ink

in his nails

& into

the slit

in my night clothes.

FAMILY ALBUM

XVII. Landslide

Father they crown

son king

of your rust

but forget

in the fanfare

this means he rules everything

POSTCARD

Saw the Nobel Prize a big chunk
little Debbie of gold

was stuck in its face the Empire
State Building a man

name's Enrique he showed me
'97 Deborah Jean's

when they gave it away a man
I lost his name

but they promise me his heart
mother be proud

they promise me like a handful
of dimes his heart

was crisp as the nickels I earned
you today well look

at me with shine in my feathers
your youngest finch

Debs & sucking down worms
with the fat cluckers

FAMILY ALBUM

XVIII. Prowl

In the wood
white debutante
you go weak
like a snot rag
& son tries
not to fill you
with pitch

BOUQUET

God said I tasted that low wind again.

Like the cork taint and ladybirds of a poor man's bordeaux.

Or the musk of a girl fucking herself on Rue d'Aboukir.

That's how my bouquet tastes I'm a bachelor.

When I'm starching my collar.

Or I'm blacking my boots.

Or I'm trimming my bale for my birthday.

God says I taste that low wind again like a breath of disgrace.

•

God said a few words about the woman I want to wife.

She tastes like my wife but she isn't.

She's fromage and baguette and ham in her mouth.

And she wears her black négligée and bouffant.

Proud like the Croix de Guerre's a brooch in her breast.

She's a minx on gin she's a gin sling isn't she.

She's liberty leading nobody.

And she tastes (when she talks) like she fucks (like my wife).

Like a nom de plume on my tongue that means *you're disgrace*.

God says her hands on the headboard tonight like she's beating down Sainte-Chapelle's door.

God says I dick her and pluck the strays from her scalp.

Saying she wifes me.

She wifes me not.

•

Well I'm rifling through trash for my royalty check when I tasted that low wind again.

The sun look at the sun it's fucking my face.

My pocketfuls of sweat and my magnum.

God says I'm a poor man's Meursault.

God said I wrote a line in which two gray hairs from the woman I want to wife's scalp.

They glinted in the false dawn like chain stitch.

And New York god said look at New York they bought every word.

And the editors mailed me my poor man's paycheck.

A crisp bill in god we trust on its haunch.

And god said I chucked it.

Along with the fingernails shoelaces rubbers snot dead skin and q-tips into the trash.

God said this is how you'll remember me.

Your husband du jour rooting through trash like he's royalty.

Rifling through coffee grounds to buy his wife flowers and he tasted that low wind again.

•

God said a few words about the man you want to husband.

I look like myself but I'm not.

I'm blouse crumbs and clingstones and pits in the shape of a man.

And I taste (when I talk) like I look (like I fuck) like myself.

Like disgrace.

I'm cat piss and flint corn and chalk nobody can breathe.
And when I shower with god.
Who dictates my thoughts.
I think of my wives and tug at my garbage like I'm trying to dismember a hay bale.
This too is a prayer I ask god is it not.
And god takes my face in god's hands and third knuckles deep.
Digs god's pinkies into each of my sockets.
Like god's trying to scoop out the oyster meat.
What you want is to return to the track with your magnum.
My magnum of bordeaux and a bouquet of gladiolas god tells me I'm thinking.
I want to chase god's women into miles.
All the wives.
I want to taste the low wind that bays when they shudder their god-fearing thighs.
And think of God's red faces.
And think of God's tits.
And think of God's every wife.
I want to chase them and pluck her and rifle through her musk.
And god says I belong here like coffee grounds in the trash.
Chasing the women.
That's not dogging around god says.
That's your vocation.
And nobody believes no matter what god tells her.
That I taste that low wind again and I'm not her husband.

FAMILY ALBUM

XIX. Disunion

& her mouth like a saw pit

son's queen

she wouldn't

shut up

so what if

son shovels

her deep

in his faces

& spits out the silence like

melon seed

TREATY

Then I lost you against myself like a game of baroness.
The last king was buried. I couldn't collapse the stack.
And the bird with the smearing of ash across her breast.
She ate what was left of my seed and named me the last.
The last of the broke, she laughed, the last of the broke.
Then I lost you in spite of myself like a rigged election.
How white, I began, and the president died in the grass.
How white, I alleged, and his statue opened its mouth.
He spat out his chew and showed me his wooden teeth.
Say you're a warhawk, he laughed. Say you want a war.
Then I lost you including myself like a forged signature.
Like a man stacking cards. Like the last king is buried.
A man stacking cards who won't say what he's building.
How white his face when the last of the broke collapses.
How white the smoke that escapes the gunman's barrel.

THUNDERHEAD

There in the field:

the olives.

•

Warm yourself they say no leave us to our pits

•

& the sky she's trying to slug herself

into the orchard

with her beard of bright crumbs

•

There in the delta:

the mallards.

•

It's the end of a few gods there's washing of flanks

•

Your breath wools.

•

Your breath wools.

•

We find ourselves guilty of our pits

•

& now the family turns south

the warbirds

their long feathers that dig out
the furrows

& trail the dismay

POEM IN THREE DEATHS

I would like to dislocate my body tonight it is small

the rain
it builds a wall around me

beyond which there is nothing

save the shack
where your father when he fell

broke his neck not unlike the youngest Greek

to survive the man-eating
giants his name was

Elpenor he climbed the roof with a yawp in his lungs

with wine
in his blood he thought

he would raise his fist in place of the sun but then slept

dreamt nothing
forgot when he woke

where he was he fell broke his neck yes it stunk

of dead corn and dirt
the sun had burned the water from

it dried the wine

the blood on the face
of the rock where your father

when he fell

broke his neck should we mark the earth with an oar

should we haul off
and insult the sun

perhaps the rain will build a wall around him

beyond which
there is nothing now your father grows silent

I would like to

dislocate my body
tonight Elpenor

HOROSCOPE

Waste of a man, says the little god who stands in my doorway this morning, *get out of bed.*
That wormwood seed you call your heart can't keep you from the work you begin today.
Let's see your poor excuse for a body, your old man's beat up walking stick of a body.
Today you will face down yourself in the mirror and say, None of this belongs to me.
You will desecrate your body and when you are through, you will desecrate it again.
A hermit crab crawling into a soda can, you will crawl inside your shadow and walk.
Today you will shout from your rooftop, Women of New York City, lay down your hair.
Lay down your damaged hair at my doorstep, like a pile of sawdust on a factory floor.
Like a pile of hay in a barn in a novel, I will love you with my eyes but must continue.
I have gods to destroy for the little god who watches over me these dog days mornings.
And today I must dream of two hairs on a woman's head turning gray on a pillow in Paris.
You will dream of a man, the little god says. You will dream of steel wool in his hands.
Today your work is you dream of a man threading wool through your woman's hair.
You will divide your body into two failing countries and unite them under one flag.
You will steal the flag from your neighbor, from his mountain of stoop sale mattresses.
You will kiss his shoe and say, It has no tongue. Kiss his needle and say, It has no eye.
Kiss the hands of his son, who knocks you down in the street on your way out the door.
You will climb to the top of the mountain. You will place the flag inside your mouth.
All of this is free, it will read. You'll say, None of this belongs to what doesn't belong to me.

FAMILY ALBUM

XX. Victory day

Son's friends
who refuse
to build wives

in the badlands

will you please
do the honors
& start washing

ashore please

HIS ESCAPE

The toughs shot the streetlight outside the clink with a pellet gun

•

They watched us go missing

•

Your bloodhounds

•

Your bloodhounds we watched them go blind

•

Nobody saw her

•

With keys in her hair unrest me

•

The rich lay like knuckles of flint corn asleep in their husks

FAMILY ALBUM

XXI. Sawdust

Queen of mine

writes son

& zero hands

mother look

on his pistol

I'll scratch

this word dirt

in the face

just this once

of my windmill

to be certain

my kingdom

when I sign

her away

to your people

to be certain

your name

I don't speak

your name once

when I leave you

POEM FOUR YEARS TOO LATE

When a man with no memory goes out looking for a woman.
When he throws his boots in the fire the night he leaves.
When he walks the wood to the wood where she was born.
When the wood's as empty as his head was when he left it.
When it's winter and the burdocks catch in his beard.
When the snow falls from the sky but the sky isn't there.
When the snow touches the wood and the wood disappears.
When he calls their names but his footprints won't follow.
When he eats a handful of snow and feels like a kid again.
When he asks himself what year was it when I forgot.
When I forgot I wasn't a man and started to tell myself.
When I started to tell myself the story I'm telling myself.
When the girl in the story her footprints won't follow.
When her name's as empty as the wood where I was born.
When her hair fell like snow when snow falls into a fire.
When a man with no memory goes out looking for a woman.

FAMILY ALBUM

XXII. Fugue

From your chin
tweeze by tweeze
mother plucking
your whiskers
now our names
son you wheeze
help me peel them

LES FAUVES

Danniel I'll smear
dog blood
in your eyes
if I have to
and sorry
our bodies
grow fur
mine's gray
and pelted
you're slate
our flanks
sorry raw
they smoke
the sundown
long & kid
don't die
like our Opa
our American
toad who
scraped teeth
all his life

then croaked
no let's run
bang our head
on this rock
and the scrub
grass in our
village licking
your meat
yes the sun
smokes them too
bang our head
don't let's wait
tie your rope
around a tornado
why don't we

FAMILY ALBUM

XXIII. Briefcase

And off

into the heart

of our American

white collar

pheasant hunt

my family

you're the first

shot I fire

POEM FOR A SEVEN HOUR FLIGHT

So long I said my friends when next you hound me

like a man in love

missing fingers

I will raise my gloves

a man who beat the schadenfreude out of the storm before the storm beat me

My friends like a hook

like a verse

my friends like a chorus stay with me

If I say it was like beating the dust from a rug with a rolling pin will you hound me

•

A voice like   *first you must pass*

A voice like Charlie sang it

first you must pass a woman

like Charlie sang it must pass

a woman her eyes like the eyes

must have sang it a woman

her eyes like the eyes of a dog

must pass Charlie sang it a voice

like the eyes of a dog when it cries

must have sang it a voice

when it cries to be let out of doors

was it the chorus a voice like

first you must pass a woman

Charlie was it the verse

her eyes like the eyes of a dog

when it cries Charlie a voice

when it cries to be let out of doors

was it mine you must pass

a woman her eyes like the eyes of a dog when it cries to be let out of doors

•

And Camus has been dead

who wrote

this very heart of mine which will forever remain indefinable to me

two years dead

wrote Ted Berrigan in the winter of nineteen sixty-two to his wife

Already my friends I can taste

the flour on her fingers already

I feel the sun will not debut

You make my blunders Ted you say love so often the word is a slip knot you thrash
inside it the knot clenches

...that I loved you before my life

...that I loved you in Pat and Anne and in Dick

And Alex back home in the city his hands at his eyelids like two broken dials should I
take them apart

he wonders and start

cutting wires

•

Or I am the trees in Brueghel

do you know the trees

Everything I have to say about working my way to your heart I say with my branches

Or I am the crow in Brueghel
do you know the crow

It is good the lord will die soon I say to my friends and they fly from the breaking wheel

Or I am the bride in Brueghel
have you seen the bride

Put on your poor shoes and rip off the door have you seen my paper crown it is beautiful

Or I am the hounds in Brueghel
do you know the hounds

Here is the single fox I have killed will you wear it around your shoulders are you ashamed

Or I am the beggar in Brueghel
do you know the beggar

Gladly I will wash my face in the dirt to inscribe my name in this stone so long as you rule it

Or I am the cow in Brueghel
do you know the cow

My eyes are black and isinglass I trample in this sentence one hoof further into madness

Or I am the child in Brueghel
do you know the child

This bag over my head I reach to touch among the screaming another who will wear this bag

•

My friends like a hook my hounds like the voice of Charlie Feathers stay with me

Like a man in love

how will I tell you tonight
Tonight the years below me the fire turned my city a bed of coals we began our ascent

and a man on his one good hand

did not wish the fire fiction

My friends like a verse like the flour already I can taste it on her fingers stay with me

Like a man in love

how will I tell her today
Today my life before me the fire turned your city a bed of coals I begin my descent

and a man on his one good hand

wishes the fire stay with me

•

Past the motherless one the tyrant the one who put fear in the hounds

past the ambushed one the fortunate one the only words she knew *I will* past the slated one is she bathing her boys in the false dawn is she thirsty

past the gaptooth one stuck forever in a theater in a blackout in winter

past the disappeared the stalked one wringing spoiled wine from a lung

past the shatterproof one in her breast the stakes of how many settlers

past the looted one the ransacked one her mouth like a sucked-out rind

past the one who bought fiction so long as it ended with ships sunk

past the fatherless one she burned off her clothes the body was soldered

past the weathered one like a hand into camphor she passed through life

past the firebrand the cussed one knocking out teeth while she bucked

past the one bred of colts her emptiest face evicted a bird from the aerie

past the childless one she said in the suite my belly it's sand and it smolders

past the breeched one her allegiance to nothing unless you count nothing

past the perdition the bitten one the one who fed hounds from her hand

past the one in refusal of death I will die a face burned into your tongue

past the mother in sackcloth the one unbidden her only lesson a blunder

        singing first you must pass

•

Like a man in love

I gut the night I am answerless I flail in my redness toward you like a nerve

Son of no man who cancels himself to hazard himself through me

Son of no woman who strikes herself from a sentence no man can write

I write on god's face while he sleeps I write canceled I box his ears when I wake him

Lord of nothing my tie see is houndstooth the knot see is windsor I gut the night toward
my love like a run in her stockings

She's the daughter of no man worth only his silence to what he can't speak

She's the daughter of no woman who barricades herself in the house with no battering ram

Like a man in love

Do not forget me when I stand at your door and occur and end and occur

Do not forget me I'm the storm in Brueghel do you know the storm I break toward you

My friends will you howl when the sun does not debut

My friends will you hound me like a hook in my mouth stay with me

Do not forget me say he ate one crumb of this woman's name and was king

Do not forget me say and then my friend he outlawed kings

Like a man in love

Fugitive when you call me fugitive

say so to say flight

Say so to say we have fled our gasoline towns

Say so to say fugitive our flight presses as far as you can throw a stone

and fugitive the earth is everywhere stones

Like a man in love

is everywhere a heart indefinable to me and a fire that isn't fiction

is everywhere my friends their hands dismantling themselves like matryoshkas

is everywhere Charlie sang it convincing myself your face exists where it isn't

is everywhere do not say love do not pull the word like a hair from your tongue

Like a man in love

They will hound you fugitive they will say where is your band of white silver

Fugitive where is his name you took like a punch

To which like a woman in love will you say I am wearing it see my ring is a ring of flour already he can taste it on my finger

Like a man in love

In the myth I break like your voice when you sing like a hook stay with me

In my life I died a man no man could answer I gutted the night

Like a man in love

I gutted the night I sewed your name through it to stay its insides from falling

NOTES

The book's epigraph is composed of lines from Frank Stanford and James Merrill.

"His Induction" and "His Escape" are collaborations with Osip Mandelstam, who died in the Gulag in 1938.

"When a Thief Dies" and "Thunderhead" are collaborations with Federico Garcia Lorca, who was shot in the Fuente Grande in 1938.

"Whole Foods" is for Micah Gertzog.

"Ledger" borrows historical facts from the Anti-Rent War, a 19th century uprising in Delaware County in which tenant farmers, unable to afford leases on the lands they rented, disguised themselves in calico dresses and leather masks and revolted. The incident came to a head when Osmon N. Steele, undersheriff of Delaware County, was shot and killed. The poem also refers variously to young men with whom I grew up in Delaware County.

"Little Wheel" borrows from the life of Vladimir Mayakovsky as well as his book *I, Myself*. A literal translation of the word *roulette* is "little wheel." The poem is for Alex Dimitrov.

"A Woman in the Sun" is based in part on Edward Hopper's 1930 painting *Cobb's Barn and Distant Houses*.

"Telegram" takes a fragment from William Blake's "America: A Prophecy."

"Ulitskaya" is based in part on a story told to an American audience by Russian novelist Ludmila Ulitskaya in New York City.

In "Poem for a Seven Hour Flight," the refrain, "like a man in love," comes from the Charlie Feathers song "The Man in Love." The poem also takes lines from Albert Camus and the letters of Ted Berrigan to Sandy Berrigan.

Grateful acknowledgement is made to the following journals, in which some of these poems first appeared:

Asymptote: "Bouquet," "Ulitskaya"
BOMB: "Ledger (Delaware Boys)"
Boston Review: "Poem for Four Years"
Branch: "Work's End"
Bushwick Sweethearts: two poems from *Family Album*
Crush: three poems from *Family Album*
Crazyhorse: "Genealogy," "Telegram"
The Collagist: "Inscription (Vault)"
Colorado Review: "Bildungsroman (Spare American)"
Drunken Boat: "Lullaby (Coup)"
Esque: "Treaty"
Fence: "Nectarines"
Fou: "Postcard," "When a Thief Dies," "His Escape"
Guernica: "His Induction"
Gulf Coast: "Correction"
Handsome: "Alibi (Honeylocust)"
jublilat: seven poems from *Family Album*
I am a natural wonder: "Myth"
Indiana Review: "Ivory"
La Petite Zine: "Analysis (Rorschach)," "Poem in Three Deaths"
Maggy, Occupy Writers: "Itinerary (New Colossus)"
Paperbag: "Poem for a Seven Hour Flight"
Poetry: "A Woman in the Sun"
The Paris-American: "Whole Foods," "Les Fauves," "Poem Four Years Too Late"
Spinning Jenny: "Little Wheel," "Horoscope"
Tin House: "My Life in Absentia," "Thimblerigger"
The Volta: "Thunderhead"

Family Album was released as a chapbook by Poor Claudia in 2013.

"Postcard" and "Spider Vein" were published as part of a limited edition pamphlet by Greying Ghost Press. A line from "Bouquet" was published as a broadside by Singing Saw Press, in collaboration with Erik Schoonebeek.

I need to thank the following people, and I can never thank the following people enough: Brenda Shaughnessy, Allyson Paty, Timothy Donnelly, Johanna Sluiter, Alex Dimitrov, Tyler Weston Jones, Lisa Ciccarello, Rob Spillman, Melissa Broder, Lynn Melnick, Monica Ferrell, David Ainsworth, Caitlin Kaufman, Beth Harrison, Eileen Myles, Sarah V. Schweig, Geoffrey G. O'Brien, Bill Wadsworth, Craig Morgan Teicher, Maggie Nelson, Stacey Tran, Travis Meyer, Soren Stockman, Alina Gregorian, Zachary Pace, Tom Healy, Marshall Scheuttle, Sara Renee Marshall, Heather Hartley, Natalie Eilbert, Lily Ladewig, Micah Gertzog, Anna Janiszewski, Matthew Dickman, Meghan DellaCrosse, Lee Schlesinger, CJ Evans, Matthew Zingg, Elizabeth Zuba, Jay Silva, Hunter Phelps, Emmanuel Cruz and everyone at Suburbia, DJ Dolack, Caitlyn Barrick, Marta Barensfeld, Emily DiRienzo, Vern Heinegg, Kellin Rowlands, Shawnee Sanders, Zach Whitney, Karrie Cornell, Dolan Morgan, Keely Guiliano, Catherine Barnett, Michael Lockwood, Zachary Schomburg, Drew Swenhaugen, Stefan Janiszewski, Alma, Alyssa, Max and *The American Reader*, Paul W. Morris, Bertha Rogers, Jordan DeBor, Ben Sisto, Nick Frandsen, Joe DeLuca, Carl Annarummo, Tyler Gobble & Layne Ransom, Stephanie Finger, Travis Holloway, my family, my friends in the Catskills, Brooklyn, and Portland, and KMA Sullivan. This book is not in your hands without each one of you.

Danniel Schoonebeek is the author of *American Barricade.* His work has appeared in *Poetry*, *Tin House*, *Fence*, *Boston Review*, *BOMB*, *Indiana Review*, *jubilat*, *Guernica*, *Denver Quarterly*, *Colorado Review*, *Gulf Coast*, and elsewhere. A recipient of residencies and fellowships from Poets House, the Juniper Institute, Summer Literary Seminars, and Oregon State University, he writes a column on poetry for *The American Reader*, hosts the Hatchet Job reading series in Brooklyn, and edits the PEN Poetry Series.

COVER DESIGN BY ALBAN FISCHER
INTERIOR ART: "UNTITLED" 2003-2005 © GREGORY CREWDSON. COURTESY GAGOSIAN GALLERY
PHOTO FOR EXTERIOR COVER AND TITLES: "UNTITLED" © FOLKERT GORTER

FIRST EDITION, 2014
ISBN 978-1-936919-25-3
PRINTED IN THE UNITED STATES OF AMERICA

PUBLISHED BY YESYES BOOKS
1232 NE PRESCOTT STREET
PORTLAND, OR 97211
YESYESBOOKS.COM

ALSO FROM YESYES BOOKS

If I Should Say I Have Hope by Lynn Melnick

Boyishly by Tanya Olson

The Youngest Butcher in Illinois by Robert Ostrom

I Don't Mind If You're Feeling Alone by Thomas Patrick Levy

Panic Attack, USA by Nate Slawson

Man vs Sky by Corey Zeller

Frequencies: A Chapbook and Music Anthology, Volume I
[SPEAKING AMERICAN BY BOB HICOK, LOST JULY BY MOLLY GAUDRY, AND BURN BY PHILLIP B. WILLIAMS PLUS DOWNLOADABLE MUSIC FILES FROM SHARON VAN ETTEN, HERE WE GO MAGIC, AND OUTLANDS]

VINYL 45s

A PRINT CHAPBOOK SERIES

Pepper Girl by Jonterri Gadson

Bad Star by Rebecca Hazelton

Still, the Shore by Keith Leonard

Please Don't Leave Me Scarlett Johansson by Thomas Patrick Levy

No by Ocean Vuong

POETRY SHOTS

A DIGITAL CHAPBOOK SERIES

The Blue Teratorn by Dorothea Lasky
[ART BY KAORI MITSUSHIMA]

Toward What Is Awful by Dana Guthrie Martin
[ART BY GHANGBIN KIM]

My Hologram Chamber Is Surrounded by Miles of Snow by Ben Mirov
[IMAGES BY ERIC AMLING]

Nocturne Trio by Metta Sáma
[ART BY MIHRET DAWIT]

How to Survive a Hotel Fire by Angela Veronica Wong
[ART BY MEGAN LAUREL]